THE
INFLUENCE OF CELTIC
UPON MEDIAEVAL ROMANCE

by
ALFRED NUTT

AMS PRESS
NEW YORK

809
N976c

Popular Studies in Mythology Romance & Folklore

No. I ❧ Celtic and Mediæval Romance by Alfred Nutt Author of "Studies on the Legend of the Holy Grail"

Second Edition

Published by David Nutt, at the Sign of the Phœnix, Long Acre, London

1904

Library of Congress Cataloging in Publication Data

Nutt, Alfred Trübner, 1856-1910.
  The influence of Celtic upon mediaeval romance.

  Reprint of the 1904 ed. which was issued as no. 1 of
Popular studies in mythology, romance and folklore.
  First published in 1899 under title Celtic and
mediaeval romance.
  Bibliography: p.
  1. Romances--History and criticism. 2. Celtic
literature--History and criticism. I. Title.
II. Series: Popular studies in mythology, romance and
folklore, no. 1.
PB1097.N8 1972   809   73-139164
ISBN 0-404-53501-1

Reprinted from the edition of 1904, London
First AMS edition published in 1972
Manufactured in the United States of America

International Standard Book Number:
Complete Set: 0-404-53500-3
Volume 1: 0-404-53501-1

AMS PRESS INC.
NEW YORK, N. Y.   10003

THE INFLUENCE OF CELTIC UPON MEDIÆVAL ROMANCE

BY

ALFRED NUTT

AUTHOR OF
"STUDIES ON THE LEGEND OF THE HOLY GRAIL,
"THE VOYAGE OF BRAN," ETC. ETC.

SECOND EDITION

LONDON
DAVID NUTT, 57–59 LONG ACRE
1904

PREFACE TO FIRST EDITION

The present study was the first of a series of lectures delivered at Cambridge in July 1897 to students of the Summer Meeting organised by the University Extension Committee. I have retained the lecture form, making but one or two slight changes.

I have essayed to give a broad sketch of certain historical and literary conditions necessary to the proper appreciation of mediæval romance. Compelled to be dogmatic in my statements, I must ask the reader to believe that I can give good reason and sufficient authority for every assertion.

*The **Bibliographical Appendix** is intended to be a special feature of the series opened by this study. The studies themselves aim at giving the general reader results as definite as the present state of scholarship allows; the bibliography is to aid the student who wishes to work at the subject for himself. I go through the study page by page, and make a note referring to and briefly characterising the best works upon points where I think the student is likely to* *require help. I have also added a little chronological appendix.*

Autumn, 1899.

Beyond a few stylistic changes and the modification of a date here and there, I have left the body of the study absolutely unaltered. The Bibliographical Appendix has been revised and brought up to date. I have taken advantage of the reprint to start a running foot pagination which will be continued throughout the series.

ALFRED NUTT.

February, 1904.

A LIST OF THE SERIES WILL BE FOUND ON PAGE 4
OF THE COVER

THE INFLUENCE OF CELTIC UPON MEDIÆVAL ROMANCE

By Celtic Romance we must understand a body of mythic and legendary fiction produced in these islands (partly in Ireland partly in Britain) during a period of time which ranges from the seventh to the twelfth century; by Mediæval Romance a body of literature produced (mostly on the Continent but partly in Britain) almost entirely during the twelfth century, but the influence of which was prolonged for another couple of centuries throughout Europe, and has never ceased to be efficient in English literature. It will be shown that the later body of romance owes much, very much, to the earlier. In the first place the historic conditions under which the general European literature of the twelfth century arose and was formed must be considered.

A French writer of the late twelfth century* has

* Jean Bodel, the author of the *Chanson des Saisnes*, a metrical narrative of Charlemagne's Campaigns against the Saxons.

summed up the feeling of the cultured mediæval world towards imaginative literature in words often quoted, and which may thus be paraphrased: There are but three themes that may fittingly engage the poet's attention—the Fortunes of France, of Britain, and of Rome the Mighty—to quote the original French:

> Ne sont que trois matières à nul home entendant;
> De France, et de Bretaigne, et de Rome la grant.

The *Matière de France* is, as all know, concerned with Charlemagne and his paladins, as also with the wars and feuds of the great noble families in the days of Charlemagne and his successors. It has little to say about the world-important achievements of the great Frank—his reconstruction of the Western Empire, his destruction of the last organised heathendom among the South Germans. On the other hand, the *Matière de France* is filled and dominated by two elements which form much of the staple of mediæval history—the struggle of Christendom against Mohammedanism, the struggle of the feudal baron against his overlord.

Although the Emperor and his paladins bear German names, the *Matière de France* is essentially French, wholly unconnected with and deriving no element of its life's blood nor any portion of its substance from that older German world which was even then preparing for literary manifestation

CELTIC AND MEDIÆVAL ROMANCE 7

in the South Teutonic cycles of Sigfried and Dietrich, the North Teutonic Eddas and Sagas.

As a body of literature the *Matière de France* reaches its highest point of development in the eleventh century, and then reigns without a rival. We can understand our French critic assigning it the first place, not merely because he was a patriotic Frenchman, but because he was a true son of his time. For the varying fortunes of strife with the Saracen, the self-sacrificing prowess of Roland, the treason of Ganelon, the dreary and bloody scufflings of Doon of Mayence and his kin, were a true image of the web of war and statecraft as it was even then being woven before his eyes.

Our French critic assigns the third place to the *Matière de Rome*, the fortunes of the Imperial City. Rightly so. Alike by the bulk of the literature it inspired and by the hold of that literature upon the time, it is far inferior to the other themes.

There remains the second theme, the *Matière de Bretagne*, the subject of this essay. I shall try to show that it is, as its name implies, a body of literature deriving circumstance, form and animating spirit from the older traditions of these islands of Britain and Ireland, traditions which, whilst they reached the Western culture-world through the medium of Britain, are represented most faithfully, as far as original tone and spirit are concerned, by the extant remains of Irish legend.

8 CELTIC AND MEDIÆVAL ROMANCE

The influence of Celtic upon *mediæval romance*, such is my theme. What ideas, what visions do the words "mediæval romance" conjure up in our minds? We do not think of Rome the Mighty. Do we even think of the *Matière de France?* Should we not almost shrink from styling Charlemagne and Roland heroes of *romance*, instinctively choosing for them some word implying a sterner and more veracious touch upon the realities of life? If we think of romance at all in connection with the Charlemagne cycle, heroes are recalled like Huon of Bordeaux or Ogier the Dane, who are, as will presently be shown, British knights masquerading as paladins. No, the word "romance" evokes visions of Arthur and Avalon, of Merlin in his mystic air-wove prison, of sea-drowned Lyonnesse and the enchantments of Britain, of Lancelot in the Black Chapel, and of Perceval girding on the sword of strange hangings, of the Queen's Maying and the Blatant Beast. Mediæval romance is for us all but another name for the *Matière de Bretagne*, for the story of Arthur and his knights.

Now the word *romance* originally designated a story written in *roman*, in eleventh- or twelfth-century French instead of in Latin. If we took language as the basis of our interpretation of the word we must needs say that romance is something essentially French. Now, whilst yielding to no one in love of and admiration for the literature of

France—one of the greatest and sanest of all manifestations of the human mind—I shall hardly be gainsaid in asserting that as a whole that literature lacks precisely the romantic note, the light that never was on land or sea. The master impulses of French literature are artistic idealism, urging the artist to select from the varied facts of life such as compose an harmonious whole, and satiric realism ever directing the national mind to those aspects of life and character which are susceptible of satiric emphasis and presentation. Both of these impulses are incompatible with the true romantic spirit, and both are entirely or well-nigh entirely lacking in that body of romance from which we derive our conception of the word "romantic." Artistically, the Arthur cycle is chaotic and formless, whilst the satiric spirit may hardly be found at all in it, or, where found, there is reason to surmise on other grounds a change in the legend. If the *Matière de Bretagne* be, as some scholars have held, a product of the French mind, is it not strange that it should differ so profoundly from other manifestations of the French genius?

What, then, is the extent and what are the dates of production of the *Matière de Bretagne?*

It forms a body of literature written originally in French, partly in prose partly in verse, rapidly translated into almost every European tongue, the earliest and by far the most important versions being the German ones. Printed on a uniform plan, the chief romances of the Round Table would fall little short of the Encyclopædia Britannica in size. Chronologically the rise and full expansion of this literature are comprised in a bare century, say from 1140 to 1240.

The chief French poet who wrote Arthurian romances, Chrestien de Troies, flourished from about 1150 to 1190. The heroes of his poems are Yvains (the Owen of the Welsh tales), Erec (the Geraint of Tennyson), Lancelot, Perceval and Gawain. Marie de France had versified a number of Breton and Welsh fairy tales before 1170. The Anglo-Norman poets who first treated the Tristan story as a connected whole, and of whose works in the original only fragments have survived, Thomas and Beroul, also wrote before 1180. The lost French poem of Lancelot upon which Ulrich von Zatzichoven based his German version is probably as early. In fact, all the especially "romantic" episodes and personages of the cycle had found an abiding literary form before the end of the third quarter of the twelfth century.

But the Arthurian legend has an historical as well as a legendary side, and this had acquired European notoriety through the medium of literature a generation previously. Geoffrey of Monmouth's *Historia regum Britanniæ* dates from the year 1136, Wace's French version from the middle of the century, Layamon's English adaptation (by far the earliest English form of any part of the Arthur cycle) from the end of the century. It would, however, be a mistake to assume that because the legend found an earlier home in historical rather than in imaginative literature, the romantic element is necessarily the younger of the two. It can, on the contrary, be proved that the romantic form must have been popular in part of France for at least half a century preceding the issue of Geoffrey's History. An Italian scholar, Signor Pio Rajna, has traced names belonging to the Arthurian cycle, in especial those of Arthur himself and of Gawain, in Italian documents dating from the first quarter of the twelfth century. In some cases the nature of the deed shows that the individual mentioned cannot have been born later than the year 1080. In other words, the Arthurian cycle was known in Italy in the last quarter of the eleventh century, and was sufficiently popular to have exercised an influence upon the names of the population. Needless to say that this popularity could only be due to the existence of romantic tales, such as we find in literary form seventy to one hundred years later. To the enthusiasm of a few Italians for these foreign tales, to the chance, the mere chance which has preserved the documents in which that enthusiasm found an echo, we owe our knowledge of the fact that the Arthurian

Romance as an organised body of French literature is a least three-quarters of a century older than the oldest extant texts.

How did the Arthur legend reach Italy? This question involves consideration of the means by which it was spread through France and from thence throughout Europe. The Italians certainly derived their knowledge from the Normans, who established their sway over Southern Italy and Sicily in the second half of the eleventh century Both Robert Guiscard and Roger of Sicily had that love of song and letters which, no less than statecraft and valour, the Vikings had brought with them from their northern home. To minstrels of their Courts we must ascribe that knowledge of the Arthur cycle testified to by Signor Rajna's discovery. And as the Norman conquest of Southern Italy is anterior to and independent of the Norman conquest of Britain, we cannot hold the latter event responsible for Norman knowledge of the legend. As a matter of fact, the Normans undoubtedly learnt the stories from their Breton neighbours. From the foundation of the Duchy of Normandy in the early years of the tenth century onwards, the relations of the Norman dukes to the Bretons had been continuous and chequered. At times the asserted Norman overlordship was vindicated by war and actual occupation of the country: at times peace reigned and the ducal families intermarried. William the Conqueror, as is well known, had no stauncher ally than the Duke of Brittany when he set forth to wrest from the Saxons the island home of the Bretons' ancestors. We are not compelled to content ourselves with surmises; we possess positive and trustworthy testimony to the early popularity of the Breton lays in Normandy. How early it is difficult to say. But oral transmission from Brittany to Normandy must have been at work at the latest in the first half of the eleventh century.

Some scholars have held that to this oral diffusion of the Arthur legend by Breton minstrels is wholly due its spread throughout France, and that the French romance-writers took from their Breton informants little more than a mass of names and a few skeleton plots, furnishing themselves the detailed incident, the form and the animating spirit. But we can detect a written as well as an oral transmission. Many of the names in the French romances not only betray the fact of their derivation from a written source, but also that this must have been in the Welsh rather than in the Breton form of the common Brythonic tongue. The Celtic immigration into Brittany from Britain, to which the present Celtic population of the former district owes its origin, took place gradually from the fourth to the sixth century of our era. The lapse of ages brought about difference of speech,

14 CELTIC AND MEDIÆVAL ROMANCE

so that although in the eleventh and twelfth centuries the difference between Welsh and Breton is far less than at the present day, still it is sufficiently marked to enable an expert to decide whether a particular twelfth-century word is Breton or Welsh. A couple of examples may be cited. In the common Welsh name now written Owen the o represents a sound formerly akin to mute ĕ, and the word, written Yuein, was pronounced something like Er-wen. Now in the French romances the word is written Yvains, and was pronounced Eevañ. The French scribe took the Welsh y (= ĕ) for his own y (= ee), the Welsh u (= w) for his own u (= v), and so turned ĕwen into eevan. Had he *heard* the sound he could never have written down Yvains. A similar piece of evidence is supplied by the name of the Welsh hero Caradoc. His standing epithet in Welsh literature is composed of two words written *breich bras*, and meaning great arms : breich = arms and bras = great. The French copyist mistaking *bras*, great, for his own *bras*, arm, and making a shot at the unintelligible *breich*, turned the epithet into *brie bras*, or short arms. Now the Welsh term is pronounced vreich vras with the final s sounded, and had it reached the French poet orally, instead of in a written form, could never have yielded *brie bras*.

Thus evidence derived from the wording of the French texts as well as evidence derived from indisputable historical facts testifies to a double mode of transmission of the Arthurian legend throughout the French-speaking world — oral, through the medium of Breton minstrels; written, through the medium of Welsh texts. This second mode of transmission is not only later than the Norman conquest of England, it is consequent upon it. Great and varied have been the issues of that event; most important from the standpoint of general European literature were the rise of a sixth-century Roman-British chieftain to the type and model of Christian heroic achievement, the coalescence and flowering of a mass of Celtic fairy tales into one of those supreme legends in which mankind sums up and sets forth its ideal.

The Conquest, which left the Duke of Normandy vassal to the King of France whilst it gave him a position of equal power and influence, contained all the germs of the secular rivalry of the two countries, a rivalry which only began when England, ceasing for a time to be English, became, as far as literary and social ideas were concerned, French. The new race of kings must needs have its own heroic legend, its *Matière de Bretagne*, to rival the *Matière de France*, full as that was of the glory and might of old-time rulers of France. The Arthur legend lay ready to hand. It was welcomed much as the new family might welcome the old portraits, long relegated to the attics, of a yet earlier race than the one it had dispossessed, a race in connection with which it might seek other title-deeds than those of force. And as French rulers of England were among the foremost personalities of the twelfth century, the body of imaginative literature which they patronised was bound, on that score alone, to flourish and prosper.

It may be questioned though if the development would have been as rapid had the conquerors found the Arthur stories in the same form under which they were already familiar with them, thanks to their Breton neighbours. Undoubtedly the fact that the stream of tradition ran deeper and purer in Britain than in Brittany, in especial the fact that it had retained a closer touch with historic reality, had much to do with the vast and sudden outburst of the legend. Whilst the Norman-French poet found an even richer mass of legendary incident than the Breton lays had familiarised him with, the scholar and historian found what he took to be authentic history. And from one point of view that history was far superior in his eyes to the *Matière de France*. We laugh nowadays at the attitude of the Middle Ages towards antiquity. The nature of classical civilisation was, as we see, utterly misapprehended. But for this very reason mediæval men felt the reality of their connection with antiquity in a way impossible to us, and they

CELTIC AND MEDIÆVAL ROMANCE 17

were keenly bent upon forging an unbroken chain knitting themselves to the mighty kings and barons of Rome and Greece. This tendency is especially marked in the twelfth century, an age of intellectual revival, of renewed curiosity concerning classical antiquity. Although the fiction of classical descent seems to have arisen first among the Franks and to have passed from them to the Celts, yet the latter elaborated it with far greater insistence, wove it far more solidly into the web of their national traditions. This tendency, whilst taking a different direction and resulting in an entirely different set of stories, is as strongly marked in Ireland as in Wales. In the latter there was at least some historical justification; the historical Arthur certainly represents the struggle of Romano-British civilisation against invasive Teutonic heathendom. Some connection there was, slight and fragmentary though it be, between the society championed by Arthur and that of Imperial Rome. Be this as it may, there can be little doubt but that the Brutus element in Geoffrey's History, the story of the Trojan and Roman descent of the British, which seems to us so tedious and so ridiculous, contributed very greatly to its popularity and influence, and that the purely romantic aspects of the legend derived from their association with this pseudo-history a status and weight they would otherwise have lacked.

These causes might be deemed sufficient to account for the sudden and overwhelming popularity of the Arthur cycle in twelfth-century Europe. Of that popularity there is no more decisive proof than the influence it exercised upon other bodies of imaginative literature. The later works of the Charlemagne cycle are in detail, tone and spirit often as "Arthurian" as any purely Breton romance Huon and Ogier are Arthurian heroes who have strayed by accident to the Court of Charlemagne. It is this later stage of the Charlemagne cycle which influenced thirteenth- and fourteenth-century Italy and furnished the soil from which was to spring the romance of Berni and Ariosto. In Germany, too, we find in the late twelfth and in the thirteenth century a number of works which belong to the old German heroic cycles, but betray in incident, form and spirit the influence of the "courtly," in other words, of the French Arthurian romance.

Causes, however, existed of a deeper, more permanent nature to which must be ascribed the effective sway of the Arthurian romance in twelfth-century Europe. Neither the patronage of the new lords of England, those new and ambitious competitors for the first place in the Western European world, nor the appeal to the antiquity-revering instincts of the age, would have sufficed. What were those **deeper causes?**

The Charlemagne cycle in its earlier form was, as already said, specially concerned with the strife of Christianity and Mohammedanism, with the struggle of vassal and overlord. Under neither of these aspects can its appeal to many minds during the twelfth century have been much weakened. But when the Charlemagne cycle first assumed literary form Christendom was standing upon the defensive; in the period of the Crusades it boldly took the offensive. This fact brought about a marked difference of feeling both as regarded the relations of the Christian to the Mohammedan world, and as regarded the ideal of warriorhood. One outcome of the Crusades, an unexpected and unwelcome one we may be sure to their promoters, was an increase of mutual toleration, regard, and admiration. The complex attitude of mind which resulted herefrom could no longer be satisfied by the simple, straightforward animosity against the Saracens we find in the *Chanson de Roland* and kindred works. Again, the incidents of the Crusading wars, largely fought as they were outside the purely feudal framework in which the earlier works of the *Matière de France* are set, tended to produce a different conception of knightly requirement and virtue. The call to the Crusade was addressed to the individual conscience of every Christian man, and although the machinery by which Christendom organised itself was largely feudal, still far more scope was allowed for individual effort and initiative. The circumstances of the Crusades must in any case have brought to the front the type of the knight-errant, of the warrior to whom fighting and adventure are an end unto themselves, and are not dictated by considerations of feudal obedience and statecraft. Roland, falling alone in his glorious self-sacrifice, must always have represented one side of knightly endeavour at its highest; but knighthood had wandered into other worlds which the Roland ideal could no longer wholly fill. Another outcome of the contact between the younger West and the older, wiser East was an intensified appreciation of the world of mystery and magic. Here again the simpler tales which had charmed the men of the eleventh century failed to sustain their appeal.

I have left to the last the most potent and subtle of the causes which forcedly called a new literature into existence. To put it briefly, the patronage of literature was abruptly shifted from the one sex to the other. The poet no longer sang solely for men, but mainly for women. In the early part of the century changes in feudal custom granted to women the rights and privileges of feudal inheritance, and thereby made the heiress a factor of first-rate importance in the social and political life of the times. The student of twelfth-century England needs only to recall the *rôle* of

Matilda and of Eleanor of Aquitaine. The material and moral enhancement in the status of the great heiresses reacted upon that of all women of the aristocratic class. Throughout the century we find women among the most powerful and influential patrons of certain kinds of literature; we find them, too, actively promoting an attempt to reorganise social life and social morality in accordance with the ideals set forth in the literature they favoured. Here again the Crusades were a contributory cause. When the husband was away, it might be for years, fighting the Paynim, power and influence fell to the stay-at-home wife; nor, human nature being what it is, can it be subject for astonishment that prolonged absence led frequently to mutual infidelity, the very circumstances of which would tend to heighten and diversify the emotions of love and the modes through which they are manifested. For the husband's lady-love would often be a daughter of that older, mysterious civilisation with which he was brought into contact, a civilisation which had systematised love between the sexes into an inextricable blend of animalism, legal pedantry, and mysticism; whilst the wife's lover might be a cleric, with whom love had the attraction of the forbidden, or a minstrel, or one of the pages or knights of her household, her inferior, therefore, in station, wealth, or knowledge of life.

Thus a new literature was inevitable, and, equally inevitably, it had to possess certain characteristics. It had to be distinct from the *Matière de France;* it had to recognise the change in the circumstances of Christendom and to cease harping upon feelings that were partly outworn; it had to take into account the new ideal of adventurous knighthood; it had to give full prominence to the elements of mystery and sorcery; above all, it had to please women and to give expression to a new conception of the relations between the sexes.

These requirements were fulfilled by the French Arthurian romance, fulfilled, as I hope to make clear, because the older Celtic legends out of which that romance grew contained in germ all the elements which the twelfth century demanded and which it could have found nowhere else. The Celtic genius was reincarnated in twelfth-century France because the times were favourable; it took the world by storm because it contained incidents, personages, traits of feeling and character which were susceptible of embodying the most perfect form of the twelfth-century ideal.

I pass on to the consideration of the older Celtic world, in which I seek the origin of the Arthur legend. Just as the historic conditions which determined the nature of the twelfth-century literature have been briefly sketched, so the historic conditions under which early Celtic literature came into being must be considered.

Two great Celtic communities confront us in historic times—that of the Brythons, represented by the modern Welsh and Bretons; that of the Goidels, represented by the Gael of modern Ireland and Scotland. I shall, for convenience' sake, style them Welsh and Irish. They differ in important respects. The Welsh came under Roman influence, in pre-Christian days, some two to three centuries before it sensibly affected Ireland. Again, the Welsh had to fight for their national existence, and thus acquired a partial cohesion, a racial unity lacking among the Irish.

Great as are the differences due to these causes, they do but serve to emphasise the essential kinship between the two communities. In both, social organisation is still in that tribal stage out of which the Greek and Roman kinsmen of Welsh and Irish had passed centuries before, and had, when they came into contact with Celtdom, utterly forgotten. In both, legal theory and practice have but slightly progressed beyond the stage of universal private warfare—atonement for wrong-doing is made by compensation to the private sufferer, and not by State-exacted punishment. In both, the obligations of blood revenge are paramount, but the injurious effects of the practice are mitigated by strict rules. Both have an elaborate classification into ranks, a precise scale for estimating the worth and station of every individual. Both have but recently emerged from a theocratic stage, if the word be applicable to a state in which the soothsayer and spellwright equals the war-chief in authority and influence.

We gather our knowledge of the social and political organisation of the two Celtic communities mainly from their extant bodies of law. Our wonder at the archaic character of these legislations is increased when we learn that the laws were codified centuries after both communities had fully accepted Christianity and its accompanying classic culture. The tradition that the Irish codes are largely due to Patrick is in so far true as they are certainly the work of Christian clerics in conjunction with the *brehons*, or native legal class; whilst of the tenth-century Welsh Code of Howell the Good we know that it was actually submitted to and sanctioned by Rome.

Finally, we may note that, from the dawn of our knowledge concerning them down to the eleventh century, the two Celtic communities were in constant communication with each other, and that the communication was of a nature to affect the intellectual and moral activities of both peoples; moreover, that, except in so far as the Welsh struggle against the German invaders of Britain is concerned, they were both cut off from

CELTIC AND MEDIÆVAL ROMANCE 25

political contact with the remainder of the European world except, to a slight degree, with the Breton kinsmen of the Welsh.

What kind of literature might we look for among these two communities? In the first place, we should expect to find it essentially similar, considering the essential similarity of their social, legal, and institutional standpoint. The nature of the literature would be determined by the historic conditions. The Celts had retained their archaic, pre-Roman social organisation with the utmost tenacity; they might be expected to retain archaic beliefs and imaginings with equal tenacity. They were still in the tribal stage; their literature might be expected to reflect the pretensions of the tribe, to inflame its ardour against rival tribesmen. They had but recently emerged from the theocratic stage; we should expect to find the tribal wizard, call him Druid or Bard, a most important character, and all that relates to his dealings with the unseen insisted upon. The duty of blood-revenge was paramount; we should expect a mass of narrative involving family and clan feuds.

The differences pointed out between the historic development of Welsh and Irish might also be expected to leave their mark upon the literature. The Irish came later under the influence of Roman culture; they are likely, therefore, to have preserved a more archaic presentment of Celtic antiquity. The Welsh had, and the Irish had not, a foreign foe to contend against; the sagas of the former are likely to be more epic in tone, and to divert to the racial enemy that ardour of combat which otherwise had spent itself upon a rival tribesman. In Ireland, on the contrary, where the country was split up among a number of clans, equal in pride of birth and pretension, divided by no real issues, but clashing continually against each other in border raids, we should expect to find the heroic type embodied less in the national champion against the foreign invader than in the glorified freebooter and tribal brave. Again, whilst the literature of both communities might be expected to betray few traces of the militant Christian feeling so characteristic of the *Chanson de Roland* and other works of the *Matière de France,* this would be less marked in Welsh than in Irish literature. For the German foes of Wales were heathens at first, and when they did accept Christianity the circumstances were such as to increase rather than diminish the hatred of the Welsh.

I have sketched hypothetically two literatures in outline, emphasising their points of kinship and dissimilarity. Do these literatures really exist, it may be asked, and can we be sure they are older than the French Arthurian romance of the twelfth

CELTIC AND MEDIÆVAL ROMANCE 27

century? So far as Ireland is concerned, these questions must be answered unhesitatingly in the affirmative; as far as Wales is concerned, more doubtfully and cautiously. There exists a mass of Irish romantic literature which if printed would fill some two to three thousand octavo pages, known to be older than the eleventh century and traceable back in many cases with reasonable certitude to the eighth or even seventh century. These dates refer to the substance of the stories, not to their actual wording; this can seldom be carried back beyond the eleventh century, and for this reason. Ireland was ravaged in the ninth and part of the tenth century by the terrible Viking invasions. During this period a vast number of clerical and bardic foundations were destroyed, learned communities were scattered, MSS. were burnt, torn, or thrown into the water. During the sixth, seventh, and eighth centuries Ireland had developed a marvellous intellectual activity, the signs and tokens of which are still found all over Western Europe. To this vigorous and promising growth of intellectual and artistic life, parallel with the outburst of song and study which characterised Anglo-Saxon England during a portion of the same period, the Viking invasions put a rude stop. But their purely destructive phase passed away after a time. The Norsemen were absorbed into the tissue of Irish society,

28 CELTIC AND MEDIÆVAL ROMANCE

enriching and strengthening it. Then came a revival of Irish story-telling, a revival of Irish learning. The old MSS. were hunted up, their torn and scattered fragments were transcribed in the language of the day, great collections of legend—historic, heroic, mythical, Christian-legendary—were formed, the traditional annals of the race were noted and systematised, and the result was consigned to great vellum MSS., the oldest existing of which is the Book of the Dun Cow, copied at the end of the eleventh century from older MSS. which have perished.

So far the Irish evidence. We cannot be so sure as regards Wales. Her MSS. are later, the oldest (the Black Book of Caermarthen) dating from the third quarter of the twelfth century. Nor do these MSS. betray plainly, as do the Irish ones, the fact that they are transcripts from older ones. Again, the practice of literary forgery was rife in mediæval Wales, and it is difficult at times to discriminate between the archaic and the pseudo-archaic. Nevertheless we do possess a certain amount of poetry which may be assigned to the seventh and eighth centuries, one poem, the Gododin, possibly to the end of the sixth century, and a small but precious series of legendary prose tales, the Mabinogion, which must antedate the twelfth century.

A very large proportion of this literature,

whether Irish or Welsh, consists of imaginative fiction, the themes of which are derived from the mythic and heroic traditions of the race. In characterising this fiction the word that rises involuntarily to the lips is the word "romantic." The most casual observer cannot but notice that there is a kinship of tone and spirit between this literature and the French Arthurian stories from which we derive our idea of the "romantic." To further characterise Celtic legendary fiction, let me record the requirements found necessary in the new literature of the twelfth century. That had, we saw, to exemplify the ideal of adventurous knighthood. This ideal is necessarily prominent in Irish legend, which is concerned not with great racial wars but with the achievements, often single-handed, of the adventurous champion. Again, we noted that the twelfth century demanded a fresh and more imaginative presentment of the world of sorcery and magic than earlier French literature could yield. But this element is especially marked in Irish story-telling, the expression of a race which had but recently passed out of the theocratic stage, which assigned the utmost prominence to the Druid and his arts. The twelfth century was tired in part of the struggle between Christian and heathen, and the Celtic tales have their being in a world remote from and untouched by Christianity. The twelfth century was eager for a woman's literature, for a new expression of the passion of love. But Irish fiction is peculiarly rich in love stories, and Irish legend has preserved a type of womanhood, independent, capricious, mistress of herself and her fancies, singularly akin, if the changed conditions of society be considered, to the great and noble ladies who ruled over Courts of Love, and held the bestowal of their favour the highest guerdon of knightly effort.

Here let me pause. I have shown that the development of Western Christendom during the late eleventh and the twelfth century inevitably threw older literature—in this case the *Matière de France*—into disrepute, and created the demand for a new literature. I have shown that one of the most important events of this period, the Norman-French Conquest of England, forced to the front a body of heroic fiction, the legend of Arthur and his knights, and gave it the advantage of powerful and fashionable patronage. I have shown that the Celtic-speaking peoples of these islands possessed a rich literature, which was bound, owing to the historic conditions of its production, to exhibit certain characteristics— characteristics largely similar to those which a different set of historical conditions tended to produce in twelfth-century literature.

The following up of these clues, the detailed examination of the lines of investigation here suggested, are left to other studies, which are issued in this series—to studies of the Irish cycles of Cuchulainn, and of Finn and Ossian; of the Welsh Mabinogion; of the Arthur and Grail legends; of the Celtic Elysium; as also of the great Continental cycles of romance. It is sufficient at present to show that the emergence of the Arthurian romance in the twelfth century is due to no arbitrary chance, but is the inevitable outcome of a long sequence of historic changes which had their centre and their culmination in these islands of Britain and Ireland.

CHRONOLOGICAL APPENDIX

Sixth to Eighth Century

Building up of Irish heroic and romantic cycles in substantially the form in which they have come down to us fragmentarily.

Building up of British heroic cycle of Arthur and his Knights. The historic Arthur died in first third of sixth century; heroic poems commemorating the struggle of Britons and German invaders were probably in existence at end of sixth or in first half of seventh century. Nennius' *History of the Britons*, in which the Arthur legend is already developed, both on the heroic and the romantic side, dates from end of eighth century.

Ninth to Eleventh Century

Building up of the Charlemagne cycle, or *Matière de France*, culminating in the *Chanson de Roland*, of which the oldest form dates back to first half of eleventh century.

Early Tenth Century

Settlement of Normandy and initiation of relations between the Duchies of Normandy and Brittany, which brought the Arthur stories to the knowledge of the Normans not later than the first half of the eleventh century.

Second Third of Eleventh Century

Norman settlements in Sicily and South Italy. Spread of Arthur legend to Italy not later than last quarter of eleventh century.

Second Half of Eleventh Century

Norman conquest of England, in which Bretons take prominent part. Norman contact, partly friendly, partly hostile, with Celtic-speaking population (a) in South Wales, (b) in Strathclyde, which still retained a Cymric-speaking population.

From Second Half of Tenth Century to Middle of Twelfth Century

Considerable literary activity in Ireland. Irish sagas committed to MSS. which have come down to us either in their original form or in copies.

Eleventh and Twelfth Centuries

Considerable literary activity in Wales. Gruffyd ap Conan returns to North Wales in 1073 after stay in Ireland and holds *eisteddfodau* during his long reign, which lasted till 1137. Rhys ap Tewdur returns in 1077 to South Wales from Brittany, and may have been instrumental in uniting the two strands of Welsh and Breton romance.

CHRONOLOGICAL APPENDIX

The *Mabinogion*, properly so-called, probably redacted in the last quarter of the eleventh century. Earlier poems, ascribed to celebrated sixth-century bards, are interpolated, added to and pastiched throughout the twelfth century. The stories of Kilhwch and Olwen, and the Dream of Rhonabwy, the only surviving Welsh Arthurian romances which antedate French influence, belong probably, in the form under which they have come down to us to the middle of the twelfth century.

Twelfth Century

1136. Geoffrey of Monmouth's *History of the Kings of Britain*, first draft.

About 1145. Geoffrey of Monmouth's *Life of Merlin*.

1155. Wace's French translation of Geoffrey's *History*.

About 1150-1175. Marie de France. *Lais*.

About 1150-1180. Beroul's *Tristan*.

About 1170. Thomas' *Tristan*, professedly based on the poem of the Breton Bréri.

1150-1188. Chrestien de Troies: *Tristan* (lost) about 1160, followed by *Erec*, *Cliges*, the *Chevalier à la Charrette* (about 1170), *Yvain*, and finally the *Conte du Graal* written 1187-88, and left unfinished by the author.

With regard to the prose Arthurian romances, it is difficult to say anything more definite than that they go back substantially to the last twenty years of the twelfth century, but were continually being interpolated, added to, and reworked over until the middle of the thirteenth century, by which date they assumed the form under which they have come down to us.

First Quarter of Thirteenth Century

Spread of the specific French Arthurian romances into Wales, giving rise to (*a*) new Welsh versions partly adapted from the French, (*b*) close and faithful Welsh translations representing earlier stages of the French romances than any existing MSS. of the latter.

CELTIC AND MEDIÆVAL ROMANCE

BIBLIOGRAPHICAL APPENDIX

⁎ *The following notes aim at practical usefulness, not at bibliographical completeness. I have therefore, when I could, quoted popular and accessible works. I have added prices even where the books are out of print, although in such cases only approximate figures can be given.*

PAGES 6-7. *The Charlemagne Cycle*

See No. 10 of this series for a general survey of this cycle. The fullest popular account in English is still that in Mr. Ludlow's *Popular Epics of the Middle Ages*, Macmillan, 1865, unfortunately out of print. Those who can read French and have access to a large library may be referred to L. Gautier's *Les épopées françaises*, 4 vols., 1879–1891. General bibliographical information will be found in M. Gaston Paris' *La littérature française au Moyen Age*, 1890, 2s. 6d., and M. G. Lanson's *Histoire de la littérature française*, 1898, 4s. 6d. A summary of the *Chanson de Roland* is provided by Messrs. Way and Spencer, 1s.

PAGE 7. *The Matière de Rome*

An excellent idea of the way in which classic antiquity was conceived of in the Middle Ages may be got from Mr. Steele's *The Story of Alexander*, 1894, 6s. *Cf.* also M. G. Paris' *Littérature*, ch. ii.

The Matière de Bretagne or Arthur Cycle

See No. 4 of this series for a short general survey of this body of literature with full bibliographical references. There exists no such detailed general account as will dispense any one wishing to make himself acquainted with the cycle from the necessity of reading the texts themselves. In the second half of the fifteenth century an abridged translation of the majority of then existing French romances was made by SIR THOMAS MALORY in the well-known work entitled the *Morte d'Arthur*. The student may read it in Mr. Rhys' modernised abridgment (2 vols., Scott, 3s.), in Sir E. Strachey's slightly modernised and abridged Globe edition, 3s. 6d., or, best of all, in Dr. Sommer's facsimile edition, 7s. 6d. An adequate idea of the Arthurian romance in its strength and weakness may be obtained from this fine work, a fountain-head of English prose.

Of the French prose romances themselves, Malory's originals, the following have been printed: the ordinary MERLIN (edited by Dr. Sommer, 1894, £1 16s.); the so-called HUTH MERLIN (edited by G. Paris and J. Ulrich, 2 vols., 1890-91, £1); the GRAND ST. GRAAL (edited by Furnivall, 2 vols., 1861-63, about £2 2s.; edited by Hucher 3 vols., 1875-79, about £1 10s.); the QUESTE DU ST. GRAAL (edited by Furnivall, 1864, about £1 5s.). An abridged modern French retelling of the chief prose romances has been provided by M. Paulin Paris, *Romans de la Table Ronde*, 5 vols., 1868-77, £1 10s.

The romances unrepresented or only partially represented in Malory are accessible in Miss Weston's abridged retellings, which comprise: SIR GAWAIN AND THE GREEN KNIGHT, and SIR GAWAIN AT THE GRAIL CASTLE; TRISTAN AND ISEULT; SIR MORIEN; GUINGAMOR AND OTHER LAIS; SIR CLIGES and LE BEAUS DESCONUS 7 vols., 1898-1903, 2s. each.

For the earlier metrical romances, see p. 36.

The introductory chapters of Mr. Maccallum's *Idylls of the King and Arthurian Story*, 1894, 7s. 6d., give a good account of the historic and philological questions involved. Branches of the Cycle have been treated monographically: the GRAIL LEGEND by myself, *Studies on the Legend of the Holy Grail*, 1887, now out of print, and No. 14 of this series; the MERLIN LEGEND, in German, by Albert Schulz, *Merlin*, 1852, about 12s. 6d., in English, by Dr. Mead, 1898, 15s.; the GAWAIN LEGEND, by Miss Weston, 1897, 4s.; the LANCELOT LEGEND, by Miss Weston, 1901-1903, 7s. 6d. and 2s. The articles on the subject in

36 CELTIC AND MEDIÆVAL ROMANCE

Chambers's Encyclopædia are good, those in the *Encyclopædia Britannica* are worthless.

PAGE 8. *Huon of Bordeaux*

The French romance was admirably Englished by Lord Berners at the beginning of the sixteenth century. A beautiful modern French rendering by M. Gaston Paris was published in 1898, 12s. 6d.

Ogier the Dane (Holger Danske)

The story of Ogier and his stay in the realm of the fairy queen, by whom he is beloved, is not, in spite of the hero's name, a Teutonic story, but a Celtic one, which has got attached to the Charlemagne Cycle probably in consequence of the popularity of this theme in the Arthur romance. See No. 6 of this series.

PAGE 10. *Chrestien de Troies*

Three of Chrestien's Arthurian poems have been edited by Professor Förster: *Yvain*, 1891, 4s. (German adaptation by Hartmann von Aue, *Ywein*, edited by Bech, 1888 7s.); *Erec*, 1894, 6s. (German adaptation by Hartmann, *Erec*, in Bech's edition); and *Chevalier à la Charrette*, 1901 (Lancelot's rescue of Guinevere from Meleaguant). His longest and most important work, the *Conte du Graal*, left unfinished at his death in the last twenty years of the twelfth century, is only extant in Potvin's excessively rare edition in 6 vols., Mons, 1866–71, worth about £6 6s. Professor W. W. Newell's *King Arthur and the Table Round*, 2 vols., Boston, 1897, comprises retellings from Erec, Yvain and the Conte du Graal.

Marie de France

The best text of Marie's *lais* is Warnke's, 1885, 10s., with storiological notes by Reinh. Köhler (these are unfortunately weak as regards the Celtic parallels). Roquefort's edition of the works, 2 vols. 8vo, 1820, about 10s. 6d., is

BIBLIOGRAPHICAL APPENDIX 37

useful because it has a modern French version. Three *lais* are translated by Miss Weston, 1900, 2s., and seven by Miss Rickert, 1901, 3s.

Geoffrey of Monmouth

A translation by Dr. Sebastian Evans has just been included in the Temple Classics. Giles' translation in Bohn's series is adequate. The best existing text is that edited with valuable commentary by A. Schulz, 1854, about 15s. Professor Lewis-Jones is preparing a new edition for the Cymmrodorion Society. Wace's French version has been edited by Leroux de Lincy, 2 vols., 1836–38, about £1. Layamon's English version by Sir Fred. Madden, 3 vols., 1847, £1 10s.

PAGE 14. *Celtic Immigration into Brittany*

The present Celtic-speaking Bretons derive their language almost certainly from the British immigrants of the fifth and sixth centuries, and *not* from the ancient Gaulish population. The best work on the immigration is M. J. Loth's *L'Émigration bretonne en Armorique*, 1883.

PAGE 14. *Welsh Originals*

For a fuller development of the argument *see* M. J. Loth's article in the *Revue Celtique*, vol. xiv. (1892), pp. 475–503.

PAGE 15. *Norman Conquest*

For all questions connected with the Conquest, the late Professor Freeman's great work (6 vols., partly out of print) should be consulted.

PAGE 17. *Trojan Origin of the Britons*

The most accessible study for the English reader of this curious pseudo-historical fiction which the barbarian nations of North-Western and Northern Europe modelled upon the lines of the Trojan origin of Rome, familiar to them from Virgil, will be found in Rydberg's *Teutonic*

Mythology, pp. 22-64, 1891, 10s. 6d. Readers of German may be referred to Professor H. Zimmer's erudite and brilliant work, *Nennius vindicatus*, 1893, 12s. (pp. 232 *et seq.*).

PAGE 18. "*Courtly*" *Influence upon German Legend*

The *Nibelungenlied* itself, although purely Teutonic as far as incidents and personages are concerned, has not escaped the influence of the French romances upon the material life depicted as well as upon the sentiments of some of the personages. Later works, such as *Dietlieb, Biterolf*, the *Wolfdietrich* tales, and portions of the *Thidrekssaga* (into which Arthur of Britain is introduced), show this influence markedly. The English reader may consult Mr. Ludlow's *Popular Epics of the Middle Ages* (already mentioned, *supra*, p. 34), the German reader Edzardi's edition of the Thidrek and Volsungsa Sagas (3 vols. 1872-80, 10s. 6d.), or F. v. d. Hagen's edition of the *Heldenbuch* (Biterolf, the Rosengarten, the Wolfdietrich poems, &c.), 2 vols., 1855, about £1 1s. A study of the Dietrich cycle will be found in No. 15 of present series.

PAGES 20 and 21. *Social and Political History of the Twelfth Century*

As far as England is concerned, full information will be found in Miss Norgate's excellent *England under the Angevin Kings*, 2 vols., 1887, £1 12s. *Cf.* also, for the social and moral ideals of the time, Miss Farnell's *Lives of the Troubadours*, 1896, 6s. Among the great patronesses of literature in the twelfth and early thirteenth centuries perhaps the most famous was Marie de Champagne, daughter of Louis VII. of France, the protectress of Chrestien de Troies. M. Gaston Paris has argued that Chrestien wrote at her instigation the *Chevalier à la Charrette* (the story of Lancelot's love for Guinevere) to exemplify the ideal of courtly love first elaborated in Southern France.

BIBLIOGRAPHICAL APPENDIX

PAGES 23, 24. *Welsh and Irish History*

There is no good general work in English on the legal and social institutions of the Celts. As far as Wales is concerned, the best book is F. Walter's *Das alte Wales*, 1859, about 10s. 6d.; as far as Ireland is concerned the following volumes of Monsieur d'Arbois de Jubainville's *Cours de Littérature celtique*: vol. i., *Introduction à l'étude de la Littérature celtique*, 1883; vol. vi., *La Civilisation des Celtes et celle de l'épopée homérique*, 1889, 6s. 9d.; vols. vii. viii., *Etudes sur le Droit celtique*, 1894-95, 13s. 6d. Dr. Joyce's *Social History of Ancient Ireland*, 2 vols., 1903, is by far the best English work. Mr. Ginnell's *Brehon Laws* (1894, 6s.) and Hubert Lewis' *Ancient Laws of Wales*, 1890, 12s. 6d., are useful as collections of material but unsafe guides for the general reader.

Professsor Rhys' *Celtic Britain* (3s.) is a brilliant and suggestive discussion of the ethnological and prehistoric problems connected with the Celtic settlements in these isles.

PAGES 25, 26. *Irish and Welsh Literature*

Dr. Douglas Hyde's *A Literary History of Ireland from Earliest Times to the Present Day*, 1899, 16s., is a masterly introduction to the subject. A fair idea of the earliest Irish heroic legends may be obtained from Miss E. Hull's *Cuchullin Saga*, 1898, 7s. 6d., and of mediæval Irish literature generally from Mr. St. Hayes O'Grady's *Silva Gadelica* (containing some forty texts, mostly of a legendary character), 1893, £2 2s. Dr. Joyce's *Old Celtic Romances*, 1894, 3s. 6d., is a pleasing collection, but the tone is much modernised. See also Nos. 4 and 8 of present series.

Stephens' *Literature of the Kymry*, 1876, about 15s., is a sound but uninspiring account of early Welsh literature. Luckily, the masterpiece of Welsh mediæval prose, the so-called *Mabinogion*, a collection of mythic and romantic tales partly drawn from the ancient mythology which the

40 CELTIC AND MEDIÆVAL ROMANCE

Welsh shared with the Irish, partly from the legendary history of Britain, partly from the Arthurian romance as modified by the French poets, is accessible to the English reader in Lady Charlotte Guest's magnificent rendering, edited with literary-historical notes by myself, 1902, 2s. 6d. See also No. 11 of present series.

Matthew Arnold's *Lectures on the Study of Celtic Literature*, 2s. 6d., delivered in 1867, are admirable in critical insight and sympathy, though out of date as regards the positive information given. But with this *caveat* no better introduction to the study of Celtic antiquity can be recommended.

PAGE 28. *The Book of the Dun Cow*

The Leabhar na h-Uidhri, copied by a scribe slain in 1104 from earlier MSS. (most probably, as conjectured by Professor Zimmer, those brought together and edited by Flann of Monasterboice, who died in 1056, and was considered the leading scholar of his age), only survives in fragments, a facsimile edition of which has been issued by the Royal Irish Academy.

The Black Book of Carmarthen has been facsimiled by Mr. Gwenogfryn Evans, Oxford, 1896. A critical edition is announced (1904) by Professor J. Loth.

The *Gododin* of Aneurin, edited by Th. Stephens, has been issued by the Hon. Soc. of Cymmrodorion, 15s.

PAGES 29–31

For the elaboration of the argument contained in these pages, see the final chapter of my *Studies on the Legends of the Holy Grail*.

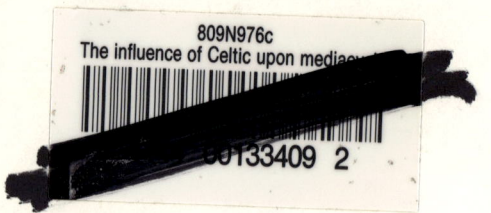